LOVERS OF TODAY

# GARRETT CAPLES

WAVE BOOKS

SEATTLE &
NEW YORK

Published by Wave Books

www.wavepoetry.com

Copyright © 2021 by Garrett Caples

All rights reserved

Wave Books titles are distributed to the trade by

Consortium Book Sales and Distribution

Phone: 800-283-3572 / SAN 631-760X

Library of Congress Cataloging-in-Publication Data

Names: Caples, Garrett T., author.

Title: Lovers of today / Garrett Caples.

Description: First Edition. | Seattle : Wave Books, [2021]

Identifiers: LCCN 2021009925 | ISBN 9781950268450 (hardcover)

ISBN 9781950268443 (paperback)

Subjects: LCGFT: Poetry.

Classification: LCC PS3603.A662 L68 2021 | DDC 811/.6—dc23

LC record available at https://lccn.loc.gov/2021009925

Designed by Crisis

Printed in the United States of America

9 8 7 6 5 4 3 2 1

First Edition

Wave Books 095

*I enjoy my drink, but not enough to name a book after a bar!*

—Alli Warren

# LOVERS OF TODAY

is the name of the bar
    on the lower east side
        where the bartender
            pours drinks for free
      after i run out of cash
  & i wake the woman
      from airbnb at
          4 a.m. cuz i can't
              unlock the door
        & make phonecalls
      i won't remember
          wheeee! que pasa new york?
          two nights later
              much more sober
        fall on the pavement
    in brooklyn
       manage not
           to break anything
              tho it hurts
           like hell in the morning
       (& my wrist hurts
          today as i type)

& i buy a book
                    at first & twelfth
          by d.a. levy
& i buy a book
          at mast by meltzer
                    & i buy a book
                              at the strand
          by nicholas breton
          gentleman & i eat a
                    bacon, egg & cheese
          & wonder why
    it can't be done
  in san francisco
          (a million reasons
                    but that's what makes
          viable travel
      under late capital
ism) & i miss anselm
          & john coletti &
              alan gilbert (tho we speak)
          & catch picasso &
    la monte young
& the night i fall
    am reading poems
          by wieners & lima

with anthony, cedar
& joshua &
that's what makes
that town the best

# HARBIN MAXIMS

human interaction's gentler
when everybody's naked. not
everyone's respectful but most

some people weren't meant to
shave their pubes. not everyone
realizes underwater basketweaving

means just the basket, hence
the high mortality rate. it's
more difficult to play piano than

drive a car but the consequences
of mistakes are vastly less
i realize i'm not made for the

communal kitchen. among the
nocturnal orchestra, the maestro
setting the pace is a bullfrog

here at harbin we're much concerned
with open wounds & plastic pants
the cold pool might make you

hallucinate, the greek salad's
surprisingly good. white flakes in
the hot pool aren't come but rather

a naturally occurring biproduct
of our water purification program
grove cabin number seven is

currently harboring contraband but
the waters are no less invigorating
they healed a cut on my foot

# SUNDIAL TONE

light plays on the planet
long enough to tell time

the bird tells time by the sundial
the sundial by the bird

time will tell the bird a tale
the sundial's never heard

a tale as long as the riverbank
from here to the hydroelectric plant

man-o-man, the bird will think
as it sails above the river

the plant is not a plant
the bank is not a bank

the bird alights on a branch
of the river, the bank, a tree

the bird leaves the tree leaves
behind on the stage

of the play it pages through

AFTER ALFRED STARR HAMILTON

7

# TRAVELS IN RUSSIA

the beds in russia are worthless though the overstuffed green leather couches more than atone for this lack of comfort. wrapped in my sealskin pelisse with a beaver hat worthless in paris but much prized here, i obtain such semblance of sleep as i'm able without a cpap (which looks like a russian word). bring me my sickle for gouging and an uber on skis behind hairy nags and i'm good to go to the carnival to negotiate for chinese tea. the byzantine forms are the only ones available to express my feelings for an onion-domed basilica blooming against a harvest moon. if i infiltrate the kremlin disguised as a nun that's my own business. if i eat too many herrings before the main course that's one more elksteak for you. the whole point of coming here is to bring back shrunken customs in tiny ziploc bags or pressed between the pages of my latest book of poems. posterity will reward me for noticing those things that escape the russians themselves, like the color of the air they breathe, the odor of a vodka-fueled radiator. on the deck of a steamer to novgorod where the oka meets the volga i'll hurl myself onto a coil of rope and get a better night's sleep than i could in a bed at the hôtel angleterre in st. petersburg. by the end of the ballet i'm sweating buckets. i retreat to my room to bathe myself in cool cigars and contemplate steel-blue twilight through the fine layer of sand sprinkled between the panes of the double window. it's for my own protection.

# WARM LIFE

the union president's dead
& they won't let transgender

people pee in north carolina
& here i'm complaining about

climbing the mountain again
the mountain'll always remain

if i'm lucky, to keep me from
sucking & only a king mule will

do. humbled by bill as he goes
through the business of staying

alive with dignified unconcern. i
don't deserve him, have no zen

no dasein, just half-a-dozen self
-inflicted wounds i'm expected

to grin & bear & like robert
plant, i do. it's like i'm in

a rembrandt or something
holding testtubes to the sun

to read my urine specimens &
—spoiler alert—i'm trigger sad

checked my email midpoem
so of course it's bad news

the ancient city is practically
gone, palmyra, palmyra

at least i still have bill
here in isis usa


FOR BILL BERKSON & KHALED AL-ASAAD

# ANTINOSTALGIA

remembering the sadness of my
life, not to mention his.
sometimes it snows in april in
minneapolis. our country
lurched hard right to never be
seen again. he was my only
friend. my red eyes gazed in the
dressingroom mirror; he told me
how fine i looked. my finger
hung fire by my cheek,
neglecting to smear foundation.
he thought i'd lost my way. we
hurt each other purposely. i
have ptsd from the bush
administration. he felt the same
way: *if only she'd loved him
enough.* we stirred flatwater
prophecies into a copper bowl,
only to blow interpretation. he
identified with me in a way
that's productive but also a
projection of himself. he

identified with himself. i was his
mirror. he was my chef, he said,
i'll cook for you. the accurate
understanding was well-nigh
impossible. i still believe in the
art he made then, but i don't
believe in me. or so he said; i
don't believe her. by the end my
vocals became syllables, mere
symbols of belief. he didn't have
to. we were done when he
discovered my name was
walker. i pointed to film history.
in reply she noted how much
you could find online now that i
was dead. he said, you're
kidding me! when? i said it's
happening now.

# EMOTIONAL RESCUE

*is there nothing i can say*
—mick jagger


might be

a bit cis

for this

but here

goes: had

a dream &

you were

there direct

ing traffic

some kind

of fashion

stadium arti

fact tucked

between the

legs of my

reading tour

at four o'c

lock in the

morning

dreaming
cuz i could
n't sleep
my lover
stole my car
in the dream
which she
wouldn't do
in real life
even if i beg
ged her to
there were
dead poets &
poets barely
alive splayed
out across c
ampus & and
rew & rose at
one point &
i tried to get
them to take
me home &
andrew's like
*it's your dream,*
*g, i'm not real*
*ly here,* but

still i could
n't get away
even losing
my shoes
to my dis
tress. the
museum was
all dioramas
& a reproduct
ion of a surreal
ist shelf that
shot tiny miss
iles into effi
gies of beat
poetry &
bob gluck &
steve abbott
fighting in the
captain's tow
er over who
se turn to
ring the miss
ion bell it was
i suppose i
was thinking
of new college

or the room
at cca with
the leslie
scalapino
memorial
bookshelf who
se contents i
couldn't make
heads or tails of
i was trying to
leave & i could
n't leave still
& you came
by with an
extremely
old poet in
tow who
broke his
glasses in
two pieces
by the di
orama &
i thought
i might
catch a
ride with

you & you
were like *sure*
& still we did
n't leave like
you do in a
dream because
it wouldn't be
a dream if you
did you'd be
awake or a
wake if you
die in your
sleep so
please by all
means stay
& dream &
finish the bour
bon ice tea so
we don't have
to dump it
& wet the
bed of roses
beneath our
feats, our a
busive talents
& estranged

principles
there was
a dead horse
stitched into
a leather vest
on the back of
a cowboy next
to the rock in
the center of
campus &
graffiti on
the rock like
*who flirted* or
*who farted*, i
couldn't tell
it was faded
out in the
drought dry
landscape
something in
a microclimate
that makes you
think small (the
general *you* of
line 102, not
the actual *you*

of lines 7 &
84) slim harpo
says *you remind*
*me of something*
*that happened*
*in a dream* &
he's not far
off the money
in our so-called
world or comm
unity swimming
pool. it's time i
whipped out my
eflat homunculus
to blow overtures
on the soundtrack
of the great work
i'm up to, said
the commence
ment speaker
at the graduation
ceremony of the
college i imagined
in the dream
it was a detail
ed dream & you

were there
directing traffic
& i was trying
to go home
but couldn't
wake up
in time
& who
am i
even
having
this dream
invoking ex
ecutive privilege
& pleading the
se fits of rage
who am i
& what have
i done with
my daughter
from the pre
vious poem
where i already
admitted she
didn't exist
you tell me

dear read
er of my
poems
you're the
expert af
ter all &
anyway the
dream i me
an reminded
me of the nine
ties when i sho
wed up on the
scene in the
bay area &
language po
etry was all
the rage &
language po
etry was all the
& maybe i even
had the dream
cuz i'd just seen
david johansen
at new college
which is now
a bar called

the chapel
or cuz i had
drinks with
micah who
worked there
when there
was still a there
there. i had the
same dream again
last night except
i was in some
kinda antique
store & sorta
knew the own
er & sorta was
trying to find
my lover but
she wasn't st
rictly my lover
of line 23 but
a composite
of all my love
rs (not as cool
as it sounds)
& i took a
mushroom

from a dis
play case
& ate it
like a deli
sample &
thought a
bout my
buddy
charlie
skipping
my wedding
still i actually
understand
he's leaving
town & com
ing back's
too emotion
al not to re
cuse himself
still that's no
excuse for
including him
in this poem
or accusing
him of my
own th

ought
s like
you do
as a poet
it's too
easy not
to be con
tinued like
a sitcom from
a standup com
edian, a corridor
in a julien gracq
novel or even a
belgian knockoff
you guys tell me
is it working
does my butt
look big in
this poem
the most
recent
dream
involved
another sto
len car but
i only found

out after i in
advertently sto
le it. i was at
tempting to gain
admission to a
houseboat (im
probable, i know)
& somehow was
prone & convinced
my opponents to
carry me as on
a litter as if
that were
normal but
probably me
ans my bod
y knew un
conscious
ly i was
uncon
scious
since
i knew
i was
layin
g dow

n som
ehow
even
as i was
driving trucks
& attending con
certs & having
to retake a fr
ench exam
in order to
graduate fr
om a vaguely
fleshed out
institution of
higher learning
was this the
dream of a
memory or
a memory of
the dream or
was it from
reading too
much egypto
logy (the lit
ter i mean)
some king

conveyed
on a bed of
rushes facing
east in symbol
ique relation
to ra, you
know the one
drerrthangbalright
this life you real
ly are on your
own & it's pro
blay the only
one you got


FOR KEVIN KILLIAN

# WILLIE ALEXANDER

deserves his own poem

alex chilton of boston

t.rex of triceratops

johnny thunders without the misogyny

moog masterpiece, mambo son

punk influenced by his own garage band

as old as mick jagger

what's lost & remains

invective against gin misinterpreted

rocknroll 78, harry james, rhodes piano

dye of a lasting bleed

i attribute my feelings to him

the way you do to songwriters

dirty eddie don't care at all

about marilyn monroe, joe dimaggio

stole taxi-stand diane from jeepster

some kinda car reference there

thankless task a boston rocker

aerosmith, the cars, j.geils

boston, til tuesday, morphine

mighty mighty bosstones

scruffy the fuckin cat

got my kicks on v66

the modern lovers, harvard square

the grolier, algiers, the brattle

a hush is holding its breath

vincent ferrini said

life is the poem

hope so

# FOR DAVID MELTZER

FOR JULIE ROGERS

i remember sitting there
among the books, how they
mean everything until you're
dying, then they mean nothing
at all. i guess there's all sorts
of vanity too close to see, by
which i mean in vain, all i
aspire to. i imagine i'd cling till
the bitter end, where you're
going out like a boss, the guy
from the haymarket riots, say,
who bit a dynamite cap instead
of waiting to hang. it's hard to
see you like this, snoring and
gasping for breath, yet death
at home is a triumph, an assertion
of personality against an impervious
world. maybe we're in your pyramid.
maybe we're buried with you. it's
12:34; make a wish, he said,
if superstition becomes you.

31

# HAIRY SNIFF

shaved off
my grief
beard

this morn
ing. walk
ed the

plank
of my
line

i'm
still
hear

ing here
in the
here

inafter
words
are so

mean
ingless
& yet &

yes they'
re there
& their

there the
oretically
means the

average
avant
garde

overage
puts me
over edge

apologies
for emojis
mes amigos

all we do's
stave off
death in

our own
ways, not
a bad way

to put it, or
what kinna
shit cannya

pull? worst
atrocities of
ancestors

*the day with*
*barely an*
*adieu*

is a line
i love
from

joanne ky
ger. it see
ms to sig

nify the way
things slip
away

# JOHN ASHBERY AND
# CLIMATE CHANGE

reading *phantom africa* by michel leiris
when i realize you're the only guy
i know (or knew) who knew leiris

i'm wading in that pool. i'm doing
foolish things you do at forty-five
and realize it's been ten years since

i mentioned my age in a poem. what's
it mean? over there can you hear?
i'm down below like leonora carrington

who died on my thirty-ninth birthday
i liked it when she was alive. as for
you, it's like a break in the permafrost

to watch that detached iceberg melt
into lukewarm reception.

# BARKING AT HORSES

marco's dog bruce died as he lived
barking at horses & hurling himself
over a balcony to protest this violation
of the order of things. if he'd been
born in medellín instead of oakland
it might have been different but if
it wasn't horses it would have been
geese or god forbid a skateboard or bike
or some other human activity he couldn't
countenance. he was that kind of dog
but a sweetheart at the same time who
wouldn't hesitate to growl at you if
he wasn't in the mood. a complex
personality. he'd lived outside awhile
& it changes you. the kind of dog who
looks gleefully over his shoulder to see
if he's pissing you off. the only dog
i've ever seen howl in joy or triumph
his comedic timing was impeccable
as evidenced by our collaboration
on the film *three poems* where he
plants his paw on my manuscript

right as i say *the script's too cryptic*
he ranks with the dogs of literature
& history & film so make room
for daddy, rin tin tin, & tell marco
we're still friends for life if he doesn't
know it yet

# PARIS WITH SUZANNE

two ancient columns to
mars in a catholic church
in montmartre. several examples
of the medieval pocket chicken
an impromptu organ lecture
a frenchman can stop traffic
with one dirty look. the moon
is sweet when it drips from the sky
tailors have fled the rue de rivoli
had nightmares in paris like you
do when you stop doing drugs
felt the futility of human endeavor
let alone my own. moss on the grave
of gustave moreau fills the letters
and gautier's name's unreadable
the oldest tree in the entire town
ain't looking good but at least one
poet lives in the middle of the river
on l'île saint-louis, like a greenway
that breathes on behalf of the city
with fingers around its own neck
they're thinking of banning cars

perplexed by *l'affaire weinstein*
unwanted soulsearching occurring
hashtagsquealonyourpig. i loved
every second there with my wife
even the scary stairs mid-basilica
and the composition of sentences
like *je voudrais acheter des bouchons*
*d'oreilles* to go to the rolling stones
we survived as a couple, different
from self-survival but at the same
time the same. a mirror too full
for words for franck andré jamme
is the title of the imaginary book
within this poem that i found for sale
at a bouquiniste amid nudie postcards
and james brown posters. they appreciate
graphic design

# HOW TO SCORE WEED IN PARIS

*Grass is very hard to come by in Paris.*
—M. Foucault


it's simple!

take line three

of the metro

to its eastern

terminus

gallieni

in bagnolet

technically a suburb

but nevermind

get off the train

take stairs or escalator

turn right & emerge

street level, cross street

through row of busstops

head into housing project

more or less a straight line

or follow the line

of people buying weed

weed is *beuh* here

(as opposed to *shit*: hash)

it's like a store

if you can get here

cops ain't tripping

they sell 20s & 50s

but i buy *cent*

just two fat 50s

but earn a nod

for my habit

& let's be clear

i mean *weed*

as opposed to the

shit hash that

dominates europe

that shit put me

to sleep but the

*beuh* of bagnolet

got me high

enough to

write this

poem

# A WREATH OF SMOKE

*queers hate techies*
the sidewalk tells me
      —noted

  but hard to picture you
    hating them, more a
          supreme
        unconcern

       as for a flea
       's opinion

        there's a street
     named *lansing* in san
     francisco southeast
  of folsom not quite
  a full block

        turns into *guy*
      *place* nudge
       nudge

my hands
drip with
blood of
what i meant
to do. i meant
to send you
a book

like the one
you sent us

spent the day you were dying
with derek finding
your book

spent the day
you died reading it

FOR GERRIT LANSING

# THE COMESHOTS; OR, VARIATIONS ON A THEME BY GERRIT LANSING

tossed upon his couch
the floating smell of flowers

the moonless-passing night
conscious of the secret dawn

roams with morning thoughts
all fresh from sleeping

the bloom of pure repose
musical with busy bliss

trembled as with excess
and heat was frail, and

every bush was overcome
diffusing light on all the world

as a flower after drenching rain
heard thunder and little after

flame blown backward by a gust
murmuring god, at last he spoke

and smiled as on his favorite isle
in a deep deliberate bliss

the history of a flower in air
liable to breezes and time

rich and purposeless
doomed to be beautiful

to grow, not strive
merely to be sweet

favorite of his rains
and thou indeed lately

cool to all things great
the fierce ingratitude

greenly silent and
cool-growing night

beginning pale with cruelty
full of languor and distaste

dispersed upon the whirling sands
blown seaward on nocturnal blast

doom makes you rich and exquisite
my ecstasy of flinging beams

scattering without intermission
ocean unto ocean flash

tender tasks to steal upon the sea
expected bliss to tossing men

bring on the deeper green
to lure into air

to shine on the unforgiven
with slow sweet surgery

to pity rather than aspire
might indeed provoke invasion

like strange sleep
the sea has striven to say

of other times and lands
of lives in many stars

soul of the early sky
the priest of bloom

the large view of subjected seas
in meditation plunged

with the benignly falling hours
to shine on the rejected

i can but speak
most human words

their sea-weary eyes
no eternity can close

as sobbing runners breast
perfect stillness of the ground

my ashes shall console
lonely antagonists

their death is ever mine
when comes the lonely wail

of sadness we made this world
the sea sighs in our brain

that yearning of the moon
out of a human womb

not eager to forego it
to elude the heaviness

through liquid bliss
i must grow old

fields burned by the setting sun
shall touch his hand

the first and secret kiss
the insane farewell

waning light of eyes
too deeply gazed in

the years that gently bend us
leave behind a wholesome memory

# NAMES OF THE TURTLE

FOR AND AFTER DAVID LARSEN

I was buying dishes in Chinatown after a breakup when I came across a pair of turtles in a tiny container of water in front of a shoe store. An old man squatted on a stool next to them. "$10," he said. "What do they eat?" I asked. He disappeared inside the store and returned with a bag of pellets. "Will they get bigger?" I asked. "No," he lied. I brought the turtles home and named them Statler and Waldorf, after the irascible muppets. It was not to be. I came home one day and found Waldorf upside down in the water, dead, his body nauseatingly soft. Statler blinked up at me innocently, though clearly the author of the crime. He would stand on Waldorf to bask, and hog all the food. "You're a buster!" I cried, spontaneously adding: "Buster Nuggets!" This was self-evidently his new name, obliged as he was to forfeit the prior one for lack of camaraderie. Ten years later Buster is roughly eight inches long and lives in a 75-gallon tank in the apartment my wife and I share in San Francisco. His lights and filter account for half of our electric bill, and I've spent some $700 on his veterinary care. He will hurl himself from any height, no matter how great, so can't be unattended outside his tank except on the floor. He's an invasive species—*Trachemys scripta elegans* or red-eared slider—so I can't let him go, and he will likely long outlive me. He's not much of a pet—understanding is limited, communication difficult, empathy nonexistent—but I've grown to love the little bastard, his drawbacks notwithstanding.

Unlike a dog, or even to the extent of a bird or a cat, a turtle has no purchase on the concept of a name, or indeed on words at all. Buster's name means no more or less to him than any other sound I make. This affords me flexibility in addressing him. Quite aside from variants on his principal name—*McNugget*, say, or *Nuggs*—a veritable florilegium of nicknames has ensued.

Buster is called:

*Old Porch*—for his tendency to shed scutes, like warping boards on a sunlit porch

*Legs McMuffin (Legs Benedict)*—for his tendency to fully extend his legs while basking

*BurgerTime*—for his resemblance to a burger under a heatlamp, in reference to the old video game

*Big Dummy*—for his pronounced lack of intelligence

*Hussfallah*—no reason; approximation of something Sean Connery bellows in John Huston's *The Man Who Would Be King* (1975)

He is also called:

*Wiggleman*—for his manner when swimming vertically, and his inexplicable dance when you scratch the rear of his shell, after the song by Eddi Projex

*Flatman*—for his appearance when swimming horizontally with his head above water, to the tune of the *Batman* TV show theme

He has other head- or neck-related names:

*Periscope*—for his submarine-like appearance while so swimming

*Boose the Goose*—for when he fully extends his neck

*Headless*—for his tendency to fully retract his head into his shell, often to the tune of Crystal Waters's house classic "Gypsy Woman (She's Homeless)," and somewhat in reference to Georges Bataille's magazine/secret society *Acéphale*

For his tendency to dwell in his own filth:

*Cruddy Buddy*

*Shitpants McGee*

*Biggie Smells*—pun on the name of the late Brooklyn rapper Christopher Wallace, or the gangster played by Calvin Lockhart in *Let's Do It Again* (1974)

*Green Man*—for his predominant hue, after a common seventeenth-century public house name ("the sign of the green man")

Similarly:

*Big Green Fatty (BGF)*—for his comical roundness in relation to his slender head

*Little Green Guy (LGG)*—for his smallness relative to human scale

*Eggman*—for he is biologically female, which I learned after five years when he started laying eggs

He has more names related to basking:

*The Genie of the Lamp*—for his enjoyment of his heatlamp, to the tune of the Mac Dre song

*Basque Separatist*—bad pun (also *Baskin-Robbins, 31 Flavors*)

*Damp Champ on a Ramp*—after a particularly arduous climb up his ramp to bask, meaning his tank needs more water

*Downward Dog*—for his atypical basking posture pointing down his ramp, in an imagined resemblance to the yoga position

*Mexican Sandwich*—for his general shape and proportion, and a wholly invented etymological link between "torta" and "tortuga"

*Floaty Floaty*—affectionate nonsense

*Ploops*—for his ability to slam his front leg on the surface of the water in his tank with enough force to splash me in the face, when he's hungry as opposed to just begging

*Grumpy Bumpy*—for his generally bumpy aspect, and his tendency to audibly bump his plastron against the hardwood floor when he walks around the living room

*Chewing Gum*—after the pet tortoise in Blaise Cendrars's *The Confessions of Dan Yack* (1929)

*Percy Bysshe*—bad pun on Shelley

*Henry*—no reason

# HUILE ÉTUDE

decade later, dozen years older
despite time's lack of existence

that form of collusion between
what we know & imagine

nowhere for a time machine
no reel of footage really

a frottage falls on reality
or at least rubs up against it

i wrote a poem called *god*
that went *we'll never have*

*giant humanoid robots*
*for the reason a crane*

*'s not a giant human-*
*shaped mechanism*

a childish thought
brought me there

an algorithm
eaten by parasites

in a third world
made from capital

a crop i'm not
due to produce

extinguishes
crude ops

at speed of sleight
of hand me ups

nobody does it
better than me

makes me feel
sad for the rest

loneliness
surrounds me

sez text from
johnny debitcard

my swallow my sorrow
my phonewallet

my lover my mentor
my manatee leaves

this still life's still life
though by nature's dead

but that modesty poncho
's one flap of misogyny

away from a cunt
of destruction

#gofigure
#whitefoxing

talked to the perp
today & he sez it's

not his fault no one
accepts his apology

i dedicate this song
to barbara york main

who studied trapdoor
spider sixteen forty

-three goddamn years
i can relate to her

cosmic absurdity
even in australia

# IMPOSSIBLE YOU

i admit i'm impressed
with impossible you
what'd i get myself into
knowing what you do

how'd i talk myself into
an audience when all i
sense is your immense
accomplishment against

my flimsy opinions
i admit i don't think
my conversation's cheap
my lyrics don't hold

weight in the street
i suppose there's worse
than me but you're a
horse of a different collar

yoked to another egg
i'll never put recipes

into poems or think
it's a good idea

but you can do
whatever you want
who cares what i think
and i'll think it's cool


FOR MARGARET RANDALL

# MY LIP FILLER JOURNEY

thank you for accompanying me
on my lip filler journey
it hasn't been easy
i had to admit to the lips
a guy was like i didn't think
you'd be a good kisser
because you have such small lips
when a guy you like says that!
i might have tiptoed
around the truth
i'm candid about
my use of injectables
but the making of the vlog
of *my lip filler journey*
is uncharacteristically fraught
it lacks the easy rapport
among cast and crew
on *my purse closet tour*
the phrase *lip filler journey*
gets 20,000 hits on google
less than i thought
though most are about me

or rather the announcement
of the making of the vlog
of *my lip filler journey*
which wasn't an announcement
so much as a comment on insta
even imdb covered the story
like they'd found five reels
of valeska suratt behind
my enormous givenchy
valeska overlined her lips
because there was no collagen
except in cows back then
*my lip filler journey*
is more orson welles
unfinished like *f for fake*
i disrupted my narrative arc
with a latenite lip touchup
some three months after
renouncing fillers and
i'm a billion-dollar business
my lip filler journey is endless

# NOTE ON THE INTERIOR OF
# THE CATHEDRAL AT NIGHTFALL

The people become faceless gliding ghosts; one is alone with the building. The place is a god. A vivid sense of having slipped into another world, in which mud does not enter. I feel the angel has a tune, but I can't find it. This is by a great, great man, but a very long-sighted one. A painted floor gives less sense of being under the feet; we locate our feet in our eye. It feels easier to walk on that water than on that floor. In the room I am arrested, a moment of vivid pleasure before the griffin. This group of toga'd magnificoes is going at various paces and not in the same direction. Rubbed the wrong way in gondola by mannerless tourists. Find myself with palpitations, a cat's fur brushed the wrong way. I find I am beginning to care for background, the crisp, puckered quality of lanterns. It isn't enough to be such an animal or fruit. There seem more hands and feet than people. People are like ghosts.

FOR MICAH BALLARD, AFTER VERNON LEE

swan feet

leave prints in my snow

all across my photograph

sinews eat their feed

northeast of breakfast is a park made for lunch

nice! audrey hepburn wonderful

a pastel umbrella, a glass of pastis

improbable cigaretteholder

not to belie high seriousness

curiosity rover hovers above us

if that's the right direction

a lil o' the ol romance

a sparkling clean room

a clear moon in a cold sky

a new color name

for norma cole

# UNSTATED NIGHTS


Unexpected but unsurprising was the outsized presence of American electronic musician Marshmello at Mexico City's Mercado de Sonora. Not the man or his music but his mask, which lends itself readily to the syncretism inherent in this occult marketplace, if not Mexican pop culture generally. But what did it mean, I wondered, to a pair of maniacally giggling little boys rocking not the full marshmallow head (also available, perhaps too expensive) but rather a more modest eye-mask version? Surely they had no sense of the musician whose costume they'd adopted. But in Sonora's terms, the meaning was self-evident: this mask represented some outlandish character on the same level as Batman or Frankenstein, a skeleton or a devil, or a lucha libre wrestler, a godlike imaginary being whose characteristics could be channeled through the mask. And the mask itself clearly dictated these characteristics, its inherent goofiness manifesting in the boys' laughter. I noticed other examples of Sonora's incongruous adoption of American figures but none struck me as forcibly as its embrace of the author of "Happier" and other unmusical turds, if only because his fame is so recent, and I wondered if the use of his mask as a vehicle for the Mexican imagination would outlast his career.

Later we were drinking street-side at a bar when a man approached me. Discreetly, like he was displaying stolen jewelry, he opened his palm to reveal a pair of small metal rods, which he used his thumb to tap together, invitingly. Instinctively I shook my head no. After a few more enticing taps, he shrugged, as though incredulous I could turn down such an opportunity, and wandered off to tap at another table. I turned to Jero. "What the fuck was that?" "*Toques toques*," he explained, a drinking pastime in Mexico, where either a single person grips a rod in each hand or a group of friends join hands while two of them each hold a rod. The rods are wired to a crude contraption that boils down to a battery with a dial to control its output of voltage. You pay the man to electrocute you. The current reaches the point where you can't let go and must shout for mercy in order to be released. Only a culture of machismo could produce such a pastime and the subculture of administrators who make a reasonable living from it.

Contrast this with the fate of the city's organ grinders. A form of musical consumption predating the phonograph, the barrel organ is so far beyond reason in the smartphone era as to be ludicrous, laughable, yet the technology has pitched its last stand in Mexico City, where decaying old men rent the decaying old instruments for a fee it seems impossible they could generate over the course of a week's grinding, let alone exceed to the point of earning a subsistence. I've read that the grinders are chiefly paid to go away, so discordant and distorted is the music of these ancient, irreparable machines. I didn't witness firsthand this alleged popular resentment, but I definitely got a dose of a barrel organ surrealistically out of tune, brightly droning away at earsplitting volume. It sounded like "Sister Ray" being played on a calliope. The grinders resentfully bemoan their increasing inability to earn money from what they indignantly defend as a form of artistry in its own right—millennials are killing the barrel organ!—embittered by this cultural moment in which people who willingly pay to be electrocuted positively refuse to endure their outmoded form of entertainment.

# TEXAS CHRISTIAN SONNET

i'll even kiss a sunset pig
california, coming home
won't you take me as i am
avocado bacon jam

i'm in the local wondering
whether it's tcu or smu whose
mascot is the horned frog
i wonder if it was meant as a joke

not meant to go so far. a cop
can be caught talking about killing
the man he's about to kill and still
there's some unpremeditation

inserted by white america
don't even dude don't even

# WHITE FRAGILITY

i'd say i have white fragility but i'm already broke. there's a pile of me in the dustpan sparkling like salt flats far as eye can see. a fine powder of me settles over aspen. too many parts per million of me cause cancer in rats. it's illegal to pick me during a superbloom or boiling water challenge. i turn into formaldehyde inside your small intestine. i cause birth defects if used during sex. at least when i'm ground to dust under a microscope you'll see my molecular structure sink its foundation. a mote of me in a hayloft is bound to cause conflagration, and i'll be those flames spreading like plague and toppling your spire. grains of me are embedded in most paper currency though we're phasing that out for the cashless class divide. a pile of rare earth fabricates me into semiconductors two microns wide in the cellphone i'm typing this on. pull my supply chain, disrupt distribution, and i'll come back like a tree disease or voodoo economic zone. thank me for denial of service and cancel my subscription.

# A DOOR. A STONE

FOR SYLVIA FEIN

*can i talk to you*
*tell you what you mean to me?*
—Prince, "Adore" (1987)

like the key broken off in its lock
or the schizophrenic recalling the shock
of years of habitual torture

or the fortune squandered by money launderers
or the lawn mower losing its teeth

like the curtain clothing a scandal sheet
or the butcher paper surrounding the meat
of human kindness or mankind's harness
affixing us to earth

(i wrote poems on this paper
and endless drawings as a kid)

i miss you like a chapter of *el cid*
i translated but my dog ate it
before i handed it in

my dog was named tintoretto
they criticized the speed
with which he rendered paintings
and despite protests dislodged potroasts
off counter onto floor

i miss you like the latin mass or 70mm film
i miss you like fotomat and tjmaxx
like the mountainside village
eradicated by avalanche

like the feet of the ashed out cigarette
remember the habitual smoker's lips
and all the ships they launched
or all the meals they finished
carrots, radishes, and spinach

i don't care if you just turned a hundred
i just want to climb up your hair

# QUENTIN CRISP

In New York one afternoon in the late '90s, I'd spun off from the group I was staying with on god knows what solo literary errand. It required a cab so I ran across Union Square to the Park Avenue side where the traffic was heading downtown. As I passed the big Barnes & Noble there I noticed a number of large and stylized posters advertising an impending reading by Quentin Crisp. The store was girding itself for the event: podium, black chairs, clear pitcher. I only vaguely knew who he was, had never read his writing, but recognized him as a TV celebrity from my childhood in the late '70s and early '80s. They would trot him out on a talk show when they needed an open homosexual, a self-acknowledged *queen*, in an era when even Paul Lynde and Liberace were still nominally straight. I remember watching him begin one such appearance saying, "Well, *I*'ve never been *in* the closet!" and thinking it was the most badass thing to say in those dark days. As I hit the corner and turned, I saw a cab pulling up. Like a movie, the door flings open as I come alongside it, so I catch the corner in my hand and hold it open like a doorman, which you can more or less do without rudeness in New York, like being *handed* a cab by the previous occupants. An older man gets out and then helps an even older man out. Quentin Crisp! Damn near 90, a bit rough around the edges—heavy foundation competing with light growth of beard—he's still unmistakably Quentin Crisp, cocked fedora, ascot, and all. "Quentin Crisp!" I exclaim. He regards me, mildly startled, as though through lorgnettes. "Yyyyyeeeeeesss?" he drawls regally, and the question hangs in the air for a beat, for I didn't have anything to say to Quentin Crisp. It was an interjection, exactly as you'd say "Holy Shit!" But I had to say something, and I blurted out: "You're beautiful!" A smile slowly spread across his face. Matronly, he extended a hand to kiss. "*Thaaannk* you."

# POEM FOR CEELS

an email from pinky
tells me you're dying
today & i wish i was
making that up. i'm in
saint-nazaire drinking
loire valley white wine
in a brasserie called *le
skipper* & the waitress
speaks english in out
rageous french fashion
& it's cool as it sounds
but i wish i was making
that up & was with you
instead in oakland. &
the waitress just handed
me an amuse-bouche
"fohr stahteres" & it's
green with a piece of
smoked duck & a flower
& reminds me of that
line by pound, *green
arsenic smeared on
an egg-white cloth* &

i knock it back & it's
cool as it sounds & i
wish i was making
that up. i'd rather be
holding your hand &
telling you how amazing
it was to know you &
they bring the next thing
which is the tiniest clams
imaginable with slivers
of toast in mayonnaise
which grosses me out
even to write let alone
eat but this is magic
french mayo i enjoy
tho i admit i don't eat it
all. i can tell you this
cuz you lived in france
& know it's no boast
more like *holy shit,*
*french food is nuts* &
i can tell you this cuz
it'd make you smile
even in death, a self
lessness & appreciation
for your friends, which
is how we met to begin

with. i wish i was there
with you but instead
have to settle for an
amazing time in an
amazing place. i miss
you, buddy. i meant
to be in touch. you're
amazing as this place
farmer, carpenter, activist
poet most of all. it didn't
work out for you, the
"career," I mean, but
christ you were poet
down to your arthritic
bones. it's more than
writing even & you
hardly gave a shit
for the rest, maybe the
smallest sigh of regret
in the end you translated
songs from nahuatl &
wrote down myths in
first person, you crazy
motherfucker! i have the
translations somewhere
i'll see what i can do
i hope i was good to you

# "ÉTAGE ZÉRO"

the elevator says to me

the elevator's a lady
according to her voice

i am learning many things
in the port of saint-nazaire

                how to eat
(learnt the hard way)

        to cultivate patience

yesterday the drawbridge
was up twenty minutes
with no real explanation

ship just sat there
                doing nothing

various men in waterproof
scurried along deck & shore

traffic backed up
a saint-nazaire mile
  (slightly longer
  than a block)

nobody tripped

  "we're accustomed to
  lack of explanation,"
i imagine they'd explain

yesterday: sick the entire day
diagnosis: charcuterie

overdose after a day in angers
scaling ramparts with olivier

(the more literal my poems
the less plausible they are)

how do the french
eat like this? carefully
  i suppose

i live in a building
called *le building*

my own little alphaville

getting emails about
sotère torregian

my own akim tamiroff

we are both bedridden
sick & alone that day

but at least i have email
where we discuss sotère
in a twelve-poet thread

what can be done for sotère
                nothing, of course

i eat nothing that day
i stay in bed. i read

                about roger stone
                back home & hope
                the judge throws
                his ass away

i read about bernie
sanders. i need to
mail my ballot
to california

to vote for him
my vote might
count for once

instead i'm sick in bed

a whole day in france
wasted! patience . . .

# GONE VIRAL

it's become like *casablanca*
handing my wife onto a plane
not knowing if we'll meet again

if by *handing* i mean asleep
in the hotel in paris while
she takes a taxi to the airport

& texting with her on & off
the rest of the day while scoring
weed with john & visiting

nat's studio to see the story
of the ear, the story of tinned
barracuda, the story of egypt

on acid. smartphones would have
ruined *casablanca*. my plane
has been canceled in this

new sense of cancel culture
i'm shocked at the fatalistic calm
with which i greet the news as if

france has been good for my
anxiety. maybe i'm just in shock
the virus has been infectious

adding drama to my picturesque
circumstances, being in europe
for the travel ban, me who seldom

ever travels! my homeland has
pulled up the drawbridge behind
me, the most bourgeois refugee

you could possibly conceive
a tear fogs my monocle, lol
like dan yack in antarctica

my problems are self-inflicted
by way of my own decadence
& i guess i'm ok with that

# PLAGUE JOURNAL

the plague brings with it
a lack of focus on what
is not the plague. vague

daydreams perhaps, like
a long-marooned sailor
with no real grasp of what

has gone. it slips through
the fingers of memory
without a grain to rub

against the tips. last month
is as distant as childhood
a different way of life

though if you'd asked me
last month i might've said
it was the weirdest month

this month is way more
weird. yet the plague
brings with it a focus

on a more human scale
scouring our biggest pot
with feelings of affection

that didn't exist when we
ate at work, ate takeout
now it cooks for us every

day. i take a certain joy
in rendering it fit for use
and the joy extends to the

task, like a samurai
buffing their shield, a
butcher in chuang tzu

or marie kondo throwing
some shit away behind
japhy ryder's back

when they were married
we're married now and walk
up some of san francisco's

more absurd hills at night
for fear of infection by day
plus i work till 9 anyway

we melt into the fountain
*death in venice* style
gasping for breath outside

mark zuckerberg's house
on fair oaks street and we
roll down quane because

it's my favorite alley name
each walk's a trip through
*the twilight zone*; it still

looks like frisco, maybe
more so with no tech bro
asshole scootering up

the sidewalk, just distant
lone figures, de chirico's
colonnades. the launderette

*now accept dry clean*
is the only thing open on
sorrowful dolores. one

night we text rod from
outside his window but
it would feel invasive to

do too often. we wave
and pass into the night
like a raccoon couple

adjusting our masks and
gloves. the less humans
out the more courtesy

on the street, we don't
want to inconvenience
each other by getting

too close. we exaggerate
our courtly gestures in a
tightlipped smile that also

means *fuck off.* sheepishly
so. we're fucking off too
kind madam with shih tzu

# LOVE IN THE TIME OF NO GODS

FOR JOHN COLETTI

no gods left
to pray to

nothing to
believe in

a time when
a space is

impossible to
carve from

most oppor
tune log

life divides
in seconds

and third acts
cut from script

poetry is all
that wires us

together even
in grief it knits

a web across
an unparticular

universe

# SOUL BOOK

*I want to write / a soul book*
—James Brown, "Brother Rapp"


bowling was my job then; this is my job now.

i'm okay with being known for preventing commercial use of my work.

i wrote religious poems in a post-religious world.

i was a complicated man.

i had a black panther tattooed on my arm.

i died in fort lee, nj, where the governor blocked traffic when the mayor didn't endorse him.

mr. green jeans was my majordomo.

i shot myself through the mouth to escape the c.i.a.

i lived among the creatures of the night.

i began menstruating at three years old and stopped growing at twelve.

i took the best photos of andré breton, except the one by facchetti.

i used my blindness as a mystique to get laid, well before i was famous.

it was easier to be ninety than marry marilyn monroe.

we broke through with a yiddish tune, then dragged the u.s. through world war two.

a bunch of us were killed because it's legal for civilians to own military assault rifles.


i died as i lived: autoerotic asphyxiation!

i fancied myself a roundball scout though i'm better known as an elderly vampire.

i endured the humiliation of mall security.

my movies were said to have high thread counts.

i wasn't a recluse by choice.

i was your overweight heavyweight lover.

they don't call me *black dick clark* for nothing.

children by the millions screamed when i came round.


despite four nominations, i never won a latin grammy.

i had the time of my life, but died from pancreatic cancer.

i saw myself become an icon though i'd much rather have been alive.

i was named for a motion picture actress who did ten days on roosevelt island the year i was born.

as a child i got publicly hugged by mae west.

i snapped into a slim jim and lied about my age.


i was a freedom rider though i looked like michael jackson.

bubbles is resting comfortably in a florida sanctuary and i wonder if he cares about me.

i wonder you.

i might've been on the front page of the *new york times* hurling rocks at settlers.

i was a sunday painter because i was busy saving people's lives.

i worked hard for the money.


i wrote the theme song for *final jeopardy* and then sold it to people who paid me to use it.

my zine was called *broken umbrella*.

i looked like liberace dropping bombs on dresden.

we was mother teresa with a siren.

i wrote for *phil silvers* and *the honeymooners*.

my brother's a great haitian poet and i spent my whole life caring for others.

i might have been barbara guest's only true girlfriend.

in this drawing my eyesight has been restored.

goddamn the bastard who killed me!

i had what you might call awkward charm perched on a mean set of pipes.

i put on my first pair of heels and ran into a nicholas ray film.

i compiled a hundred eleven to seventy record in eight seasons at punxsutawney high.

i married my husband between talks about surrealism and the latest trends.

i wasn't the only artist on capp street.

in my short forty years, i raised my fair share of hell.

they called me the guerilla dandy.

i was a two-time recipient of the yellow kid award.

i made a promotional film for sears even as i was the queen of experimental ethnofilmography.

i went to harvard law to become a comedian.


i was the julia child of embroidery.

i made my mark as a poster when images were scarce.

all i have's a guitar pick.

i would've liked to have been poussin, if i'd had a choice, in another time.

my most famous novel is a series of statements made in the first person.

i gave better advice than my twin sister.


the way the mission's gone has me rolling in my grave.

i taught the blind to tango and foxtrot.

my last location was in hell's kitchen.

apart from three weeks in nineteen thirty, i was an entirely self-taught artist.

you could say i started off-off-broadway.

i approached computer science with a kind of casual brilliance.

my husband almost became vice president while knocking up his videographer.


we staged *the vagina monologues* in haiti and led the charge to make rape illegal.

i did everything i could for women's and children's rights.

i built two adobe brick houses by hand by myself.

i knew i was gay at six years old and came out at eighteen.

you might find me in the whitepages or at least the *fresno bee*.

you might try to make me go to rehab.

our aircraft crashed into the adriatic en route to albania.

each *matlock* could be our last.

i was a table tennis tristan tzara.

when i met my wife, she was working as hume cronyn's secretary.

i was the primary architect for the temple of the frog.

i was known as *the fountain lady*.

i invented a whole wing of queer writing trying to survive.

i removed my parents from the bulk of the story.

i was a proud inductee into the toy industry hall of fame.

i wanted justice but merely gained the rule of law.

i was the first female head of an islamic state.

my mother composed many a famous creole waltz.

i sang with edith piaf at cannes.

i went out like james gandolfini, after some bomb-ass italian food.

i offered insight into the life of a prime minister's wife, influenced by germaine greer.

i left my shoes in a restaurant last time i saw ferlinghetti.

because the greatest love of all happened to me, it was easy to believe.

most people don't know *the spirit* and i think it's sad.

my nickname was *rah*, rough as hell, though it didn't reflect my nature.

after a stint in an internment camp, i was raped by five guys right before i turned ten.

my figures were larger than life.

they called me *the voice of darts*.

it hurts me what happened to him.

if you've ever waited to hear a brass bowl's last vibration then you know what i'm about.

they will only confirm that my first stories were written in swedish.

i might have contributed to the furry movement.

my clientele included billie holiday and pablo fucking picasso.

it didn't matter that i was born in hayward, i was thrown in a concentration camp.

i've been called *the south's answer to julia child*.

i worked for the o.s.s.

i wrote the book on poster art.

my plays had sexually suggestive titles.

i stole lines from frank lima when i ran out of ideas.

my wife was eight months pregnant when she was murdered and left in a ditch.

my grandfather invented psychoanalysis, which left me slightly traumatized.

i came within an ace of being elected sheriff of pitkin county.

i shared a birthday with philip lamantia.

i designed covers for lamantia and david bowie.

i was mentioned in a bowie song.

i made multiple appearances on *the x-files*.

time took a cigarette and put it in my mouth.

i'm still making art from beyond the grave through a team of highly trained assistants.


my photographs were more about me than my subjects, even the ones of paris hilton.

i found myself in the odd company of a dancer and the leader of the decorative art movement.

i founded america's largest distributor of printed material from the people's republic of china.

i mostly wrote for children because i found they were more open-minded.


if i was known as the savior of jugtown, it's not what you think.

i felt both beautiful and ridiculous fencing in a skirt—talk about fetish photography!

i might have invented naked funk.

i wanted to be a revolutionary and change this world, especially for the poor.

i revitalized the cutout and made art out of dung and diapers.

the film adaptation of my most famous book features robert de niro in a diaper.


i did for cuban spanish what mark twain did for american english.

my trademark was the braided frog handle.

quentin tarantino called me his one true collaborator.

my daughter and granddaughter became prominent artists in their own right.

they never found who committed my gruesome murder.

they say my death was unrelated to my activism, but was it?

i was expelled from school for getting married.

for much of my life i was known as *el man*.

they called me *black elvis* after i bought my mansion in philly.

i developed the egg mcmuffin as a fastfood version of eggs benedict.

the lord woke me up in the middle of the night and told me to feed the hungry.

i emerged as the leader of the opposition after my husband was killed.

i was happy to share a name with a cherokee indian chief.

i developed modernist figuration even as abstract expressionism unfolded.

ironically enough, the drummer on my second album was named *elvis wong*.

i was married eight times to seven men.

i asked, what color was it, but the color wasn't really important.

i chose the color green as racially neutral and also the symbol of life.

i knew where the wild things were.

i sang the body electric.

i played a vicious fag hag and a sex-crazed southern belle.


my *selected poems* was recently published by talisman.

my son sam's still holding it down.

i rocked even when i couldn't talk.

i did exactly the opposite of what i was taught.

i portrayed bernabe zamora, joaquin delgado, and emeterio vasquez on so many episodes of *wagon train*.

my parents had me hospitalized and stuffed full of barbiturates.

i was in love.

my partner of twenty-seven years was named tam o'shaughnessy.

like richard o. moore, i met death at the redwoods in mill valley.

i died on your birthday, bitch!


i wrote a *reading rainbow* book.

when i was ten i begged my mother for a remington typewriter.

i vanquished my opponents in a handicapped evening-gown match.

i sold erotic drawings to my classmates for a quarter.

i did for mexican spanish what that other guy did for cuban.


i found virginia woolf intellectually distinguished but rude and unpleasant.

some called me the mother of hip-hop.

as a sailor i went out at sea.

my gods were herman melville, emily dickinson, and mozart.

for a writer like me, a place like salford was worth its weight in gold.

i would have killed him sooner but the grapes were souring in the vats.

i was in bands like the skinflutes and john henry west.

my label was called hi-density records.

i was the father of puerto rican archaeology.

i raised my pflag high.

i'm the only female honky in *a great day in harlem*.

i realized equating the white race with cancer was an insult to people with cancer.

my mother worked in a sweatshop to support the family, so i devoted my life to the poor.

even after my sex change my strapping tenor remained.

i wrote the vitameatavegamin scene for *i love lucy*.

i started iranian modernism, such as it was.

i was the oldest first grader ever, at age eighty-four.

russian hockey officials called our plane crash *the darkest day in the history of sports*.

i was the most important figure in regional mexican music even though i was born in long beach.

the *new york times* described me as a *pathetically appealing vulgarian*.

i was the first female baseball scout and am currently the last.

i died three days after johnny otis, who discovered me in nineteen fifty-two.

i held my editorial meetings at the mark hotel.

if my husband had been a dentist, i probably would have become one too.

i often cited hemingway as my single greatest influence.

i got a fulbright to study under merleau-ponty.

i was the last great independent titan of the cosmetics industry.

i was almost routinely hailed as the world's greatest living choreographer.

new york was like a jungle but it gave me a feeling of total freedom.

i took the fall for dalton trumbo by taking credit for *gun crazy*.

i lived to be one hundred due to my absolute pacifism.

i coined the word *superhighway* in relation to telecommunications.

i was the first woman to lie in state at the capitol rotunda.

i saw patterns where not many other people did.

i took being called *shark lady* as a compliment.

i had an obsession with mental illness.

i enjoyed visiting area churches.

i was part of a long family legacy of preserving my tribe's native language.

like king lear i had gone in search of the truth and then i had noth-
ing.

as a teacher i was criticized for coming in too early and leaving too
late.

my bookstore was called *politics and prose.*

i was one of a handful of guests banned from *late night with david
letterman.*

i began my athletic career as a coxswain with the saint ignatius crew.


i was considered the most important interpreter of messiaen's piano
works.

my office was next to the oval office during the carter administration.

even my private images had social commentary.

my brief career was influenced by czech surrealism.

i was banned from mainland china after the british handover.

for years, i shared a basement office with bill berkson.

in berkeley i learned to make hummus, in richmond how to spy on prostitutes.

one of my first major pieces depicted a lactose-intolerant gay man coming to terms with his dairy-obsessed mother.

i invented a new form of ice cream.


i was a self-described church-going, god-fearing man.

i made many hardcore x-rated films under pseudonyms.

i unsuccessfully sued the walt disney company for defamation.

i stumbled into my brand by trying to disguise orange-juice stains.

for those who've read all four of my books, the thread is clear.

i appeared in films with zsa zsa gabor and mamie van doren.

you might know my work from *star blazers*.


i played the chief science officer in *pigs in space*.

they called me the puppet master.

i attended lorne greene's academy of radio arts.

i was just my friend's mom; it was enough.

i loved doughnuts.

i worked on your foot.

i worked for subcomandante marcos.

i worked for campbell's soup.

we sadly ignored the ancient high-water mark.


i created the commodore sixty-four.

i always had a succession of ideas in my head.

we never decided to become dissidents; we simply went ahead and did certain things that we felt we ought to do.

i almost never used the term *avant-garde*.

all great movements start in murmurs and i could hear those mur-
murs.

my father was killed in a freak lift accident.

i thought joyce cary sucked so much, i decided to become a writer to
atone for him.

the *new york times* called me *one of the most respected voices in amer-
ican cheese.*

we were murdered for reporting on reporters being murdered.

it's been said as a young woman i had an affair with frida kahlo.

i lived in a prison in tijuana by choice.

i beat george foreman strictly on points.

there's precious little coverage of my handball career in english.

i was the third-best grandmaster in yugoslavia but definitely the most
rock & roll.

i was a regular random person.

i lost my ability to taste and smell.

my first innovations were in the intravenous fat program.

a youthful foray into ballet is among my lesser-known endeavors.

my voice hit the whistle register.

i connected high minimalism to disco and protopunk.

i invented the blaxploitation film.

i was hung out to dry by my own editors for exposing the c.i.a.'s crack connection.


i got turned on to art by vincent price.

i prepared my famous epigram all on my own.

my caregiver and i spoke to each other by tracing letters on our palms.

i embraced every tree in my yard because i knew i would never return.

FOR VERONICA DE JESUS

Some of these poems appeared in the following periodicals: *Blazing Stadium, Brooklyn Rail, Castle Greyskull, Censer, The Doris, Granta* (offered money; never paid), *High Noon, Knockwurst, OAR, Panda's Friend, PoetryNow, The Recluse,* and *VOLT*. I may have lost track of one or two, to the editors of which I apologize. Rough year.

Some appeared in the following anthologies:

*Bronze Chimes: Poems After Alfred Starr Hamilton*, eds. Frank Haines and Cedar Sigo (New York: Heinzfeller Nileisist, 2015)

*Studio One Reading Series: 10 Years, 54 Poets, an Anthology*, eds. Casey McAlduff and Sheila Davies Sumner (Oakland: speCt!, 2019)

*Salones de belleza: escritores en Aeromoto/The Beauty Salons: Writers at Aeromoto*, eds. Kit Schluter and Tatiana Lipkes (Mexico City: Gato Negro Ediciones, 2021)

Some appeared in the following books and chapbooks:

*Noches apátridas: poesía escogida/Unstated Nights: Selected Poems 1999–2019* (Mexico City: Juan Malasuerte, 2019)

*The Saint-Nazaire Notebook* (Catskill, NY: Blazing Stadium, 2020)

*Pour les dieux que j'ai croisés/For the Gods I've Known* (Saint-Nazaire, France: MEET, 2021)

*Names of the Turtle* (San Francisco: Gas Meter Editions, 2021)

An earlier version of "Soul Book" appeared in *People Are a Light to Love: Memorial Drawings, 2004–2016* by Veronica de Jesus (San Francisco: RITE Editions, 2017)